YOUR CAREER IN . . .

# MARKETING, SALES AND MARKET RESEARCH

Barbara Priestley

A Daily Express / Cornmarket Book

First published 1970 by Cornmarket Press Limited
42/3 Conduit Street, London WIR ONL
in association with the *Daily Express*

Copyright © Cornmarket Press Limited

Set in Photon Times 11 pt by
Richard Clay (The Chaucer Press), Ltd, Bungay, Suffolk
and printed in Great Britain by
Fletcher & Son, Ltd, Norwich, Norfolk

## OTHER TITLES IN THE SERIES

Series editor Frances Verrinder

Cover design Margaret Stobo

Questionnaire on the cover kindly provided by Louis Harris Research Ltd

Photograph on page 19 by kind permission of Tesco Ltd

Photograph on page 31 by kind permission of British Market Research Bureau

Photograph on page 42 by kind permission of British Market Research Bureau

Photograph on page 56 by kind permission of Audience Studios Ltd, London

The editor would like to thank Mr K. S. D. Wilmshurst of *Merchandising & Marketing Development Ltd*, London for his help and advice on the manuscript.

# CONTENTS

# Introduction

Marketing is basically finding out what people want, making it in the right shape and at the right price and persuading them to buy it. It includes market research — making sure that the product is what people need or want — displays in shops, advertising on television, in the Press and by direct mail, pricing, packaging and helping to plan the products of the future. It also includes the work of the salesman and sales manager who show the product to the shopkeeper or their customers and persuade them to buy it. The planning which makes all these efforts succeed is called Marketing.

Marketing offers many different careers. Trainees usually start in one branch of it — as junior salesmen, trainee market researchers, in advertising, in a statistics branch or as general management trainees. There are three main levels of entry: at sixteen with about five GCE O level or equivalent passes, at eighteen with one or two GCE A level passes or an OND in Business Studies and at graduate level.

It must be admitted straight away that many young people at all these levels do not even consider this kind of work. There are several reasons for this. You may simply not know anything about marketing. You may feel that selling is not a job for an educated person or you may be critical of the whole idea of selling goods to make a profit.

It is a pity that these prejudices exist. Often the very young people who hold these ideas are intelligent and creative and might well enjoy the tough but stimulating world of marketing.

First of all, people generally do not know much about marketing. Apart from shop assistants and the odd market research interviewer, marketers do not deal direct with the public, though they know more about people and influence them more than most other professions. Marketing men do not make the news as personalities. Although the evidence of marketing is all about us, part of the wallpaper of everyday life, the work is 'backroom', usually quite palatial backrooms! So that to find out about this career you need to ask questions and to read books like those listed on pages 62 and 63.

The feeling that the work of the salesman is somehow distasteful is a strange relic from the days when no 'gentleman' would go into trade. The image of the salesman is only slowly changing as people realise that in order to survive economically Britain depends on skilled salesmen to sell her goods overseas.

The salesman's job nowadays is to develop a mutually satisfactory arrangement with his customer. He starts by discussing the customer's needs: in the case of an industrial salesman selling turbines or packaging or insurance to another firm, the product on offer may well be adapted to suit those needs.

The old distrust of salesmen has largely been buried; indeed, many representatives are responsible for counting the shopkeeper's stock of their product and advising him what to re-order. Salesmen of all kinds, and especially those of technical products, need to know in detail about their product. Most are not only highly trained in sales methods but also well informed about the whole process that has brought their product on to the market.

In our society the general level of wealth created by trade determines the level of spending in schools, hospitals and social services of all kinds. Marketing makes trading more efficient, more conscious of the customer's needs and more likely to succeed. Marketing is an important part of economic life and brings real benefits to us all.

The big expansion of marketing has happened in your lifetime. Until very recently British manufacturers did not have to worry too much about selling what they made. They were confident of their technology and workmanship and believed that 'a good product sells itself'. Once perhaps that was almost true. Now, however, two things have happened. First, Britain has been overtaken technically by some other countries, and so needs to make more effort to persuade overseas buyers to purchase her goods; secondly, more people in this country have more money to buy goods than ever before. They have enough money available to think of owning things that used to be luxuries, and they no longer automatically take the cheapest product when buying necessities.

In this setting, British manufacturers of all kinds of goods have started to look favourably on marketing. Many have set up or have expanded marketing departments, showing new interest in training their planners, researchers and salesmen. Universities and colleges have established courses in marketing leading to degrees, the Diploma in Marketing of the Institute of Marketing or other qualifications. As time goes on there are likely to be more and more openings in these fields.

\*       \*       \*

The simplest way to explain the various kinds of work involved in marketing is to divide it into two main areas, *Consumer marketing*, ie promoting goods to be sold through shops and other organisations to the housewife and her family, and *industrial marketing*, promoting goods, eg machine tools and services, eg office cleaning, to be sold to another manufacturing company.

This book sets out under both headings a description of the organisation and jobs involved in the planning of marketing and in sales departments at home and abroad. The following sections deal with market research: sales training officers, who arrange the firms' instruction for salesmen; teachers of marketing in colleges or universities; and consultants in marketing, who advise manufacturers on specific problems, for a fee.

Advertising, public relations and retailing – working in or managing a shop or chain of shops – have been omitted. They are discussed in two other books in this series – *Your Career in Retailing and distributive trades* and *Your Career in Advertising and public relations*.

Having explained the basic structure of marketing and the jobs of the people concerned, the whole process is brought to life on page 37 by following the progress of two entirely fictitious pieces of marketing – the launching of *Primrose Margarine* and the selling of *Storright* systems to a hardware warehouse. The direction taken by these two examples is not meant to be typical. They are intended only as exercises to illustrate as clearly as possible the work involved in the various sectors of marketing.

# Consumer Marketing

Consumer marketing aims to find out what the general public wants and then to persuade them to buy it. If a product is well known and in demand there is obviously not much difficulty in persuading shopkeepers of all kinds to stock it. Included in this category are packaged goods of many types — food and detergents, clothes and furniture, 'consumer durables' like cars and refrigerators, and services like catering and dry cleaning.

The marketer has to find out what the customer wants, make a better product to meet these desires at a reasonable price, and still allow himself and the shopkeeper to make a profit; the product will almost certainly be advertised and a decision made about where to sell the goods; salesmen must be briefed to sell the product; the shopkeeper must be provided with display material to give the product prominence in his shop.

A new entrant to marketing might start in various ways. If you have GCE O levels the first job might be in fairly routine office work, coupled with day-release or evening study for an Ordinary National Diploma in Business Studies. Some small firms run commercial apprenticeships for sixteen-year-olds in connection with the British Chambers of Commerce. Other larger firms have their own commercial training schemes. Some of these aim to help young people to qualify as accountants or company secretaries, as well as a few to become sales and marketing managers. Indeed, marketers sometimes start as accountants or statisticians. Occasionally a firm asks for an O level entrant as a trainee salesman or market researcher, but usually as a school-leaver going in at this level you start on a more general commercial training. You may then be chosen for training as a junior salesman or other specialist.

Rather more training schemes of this sort are available for A level entrants, and there are many general management training schemes for graduates. As an entrant at these levels, you might also start as a trainee salesman, market research assistant, statistical assistant or a trainee in advertising. At this stage, beginners usually combine training within the firm, either in their own particular branch or, in the case of management trainees, in a number of different departments. Formal marketing education is gained by studying at evening classes or by correspondence course for the Diploma in Marketing of the Institute of Marketing. Some graduate entrants may already have taken a first degree course including marketing or a postgraduate course in marketing; other entrants may have the post-graduate Diploma in Management Studies or other relevant business qualifications.

A firm's own training scheme for marketing might last four to five years. As a trainee you might spend eighteen months in the market research department as an assistant research officer, six months in an advertising agency working and observing, some time in the sales head office and then a period on the road working as a salesman. You might well finish in the firm's distribution department liaising with shops, or in a shop serving and assisting the manager. In each job you would be working as well as learning.

Marketing is essentially an executive career — as you see, you cannot go straight into it without some qualification, training or experience. From salesman, general trainee or research assistant to a job in marketing is a big step; not everyone makes it. For those who do, the next appointment is often to *product* or *brand manager*. He is responsible for the promotion and sales of one or more of the firm's products — say, a range of orange, lemon and grapefruit squashes. He will draw up a budget for his squashes, and it will be up to him to decide how much to spend on TV, in magazine and press advertisements, posters, displays in shops as well as research to check the effectiveness of all this. He will also have to forecast seasonal demands — extra orders at Christmas and in the summer holidays — and as well maintain a general, more gradual increase in sales.

The brand manager's can be a difficult job. He is responsible to the senior marketing managers for all that happens to his product. If he encourages and brings out an effective new advertisement and selling point — 'X Fruit Squashes give you Energy' or 'X Fruit Squashes soothe you' — he will be given the credit. On the other hand, if it snows in July and supermarket shelves remain crammed with X fruit squashes the loss of profit will affect his budget and may make him cut down on future plans. Perhaps he should have rushed out a recipe for hot fruit punch!

Although he has much influence on his own products, the brand manager is part of a team. He is responsible to senior managers and must work closely with other departments. He is a co-ordinator of advertising, sales, accounting and so on, and often has to persuade specialists in other departments to carry out work for him without having direct authority over them. He must therefore be tactful but never self-effacing. It is also important that at meetings with other executives he should be able to put over his ideas with clarity, enthusiasm and conviction.

In his middle to late twenties a brand manager can expect to earn £1500–£2500 a year. His job includes most of the processing involved in marketing work. Promotion is likely to bring him responsibility for a progressively larger number of his firm's products and more influence over what happens to them, rather than any distinctively different kinds of work.

The marketer's next promotion might be to *marketing manager* or *assistant marketing manager* or *marketing services manager*, depending on the way his firm is organised. A *marketing services manager* plans and provides the help needed by the marketing department in the form of market research, advertising, shop displays and statistical and other management services. He may have to arrange for agencies to undertake this work or to co-ordinate the work of these various departments in his own company. A *marketing manager* has to plan and follow through all the arrangements for promoting and selling a whole range of goods, working closely of course with brand or product managers. On the most simple level he has to make sure that all his brands are selling as well as possible and that they are the best combination of goods from the firm's point of view – and from the customer's. In a range of biscuits all must fit the company's image for quality goods; if there are two kinds of shortcake biscuit both must sell briskly to justify their independent existence; different nuances must come over in the advertising for each type. In conjunction with the brand manager he must be ready to recognise and sometimes create new opportunities to sell his goods. The firm's marketing managers are working with large sums of money, and much of the company's profit depends on them, so they are well paid. Many are in their late twenties or early thirties, an age when other kinds of real executive management jobs are rare.

In a large firm the head of marketing is the *marketing director*, a board-room level job, carrying responsibility for all the company's marketing work, generally supervising its direction and negotiating with the other directors for all the money spent on this activity. He might well be paid £10,000 or more, but his salary, like those of all executives, would depend ultimately on how much money the company spends and earns.

## Working abroad

Consumer marketing overseas is rather differently organised. Britain is having to export more and more each year to pay her way, and so this is obviously an expanding area of work. The initial jobs and training leading to this work are similar to those for home marketing. There are training schemes for eighteen-year-olds and graduates (and sometimes for sixteen-year-olds). Entrants need much the same basic commercial and creative instincts and on-the-job training, supplemented by formal marketing education or perhaps by study for the Institute of Export's examinations. This kind of career is a good way to make use of a language, and this is fine if one speaks it fluently, has mastered commercial and technical terms, and knows the country and its people well. Otherwise it is much better to speak English through a good interpreter.

Even if he is based on London, the overseas marketer would spend at least half his time abroad. He may well be based overseas, with just long holidays and visits for conferences at home. Marketing abroad – being really involved in finding out the best goods to sell and the best way of promoting them – means more than just sending out salesmen with special export lines. Different companies approach the problem in different ways.

17

Some have no overseas marketing department, but make their goods suitable for sale throughout the world, with international advertising and research. They may or may not have factories in other countries staffed by local managers and workers making their products. Such firms would probably use local marketers too, and a British-based marketing manager would work with them, visiting the country frequently, advising and correlating all the marketing of his product throughout the world, or an area of it. Other companies organise their exports on an area basis, having British *area representatives* in European countries, developing countries, Commonwealth countries and so on. Some combine the two systems.

If you started at eighteen or as a graduate, you would start by working in home marketing. Your first overseas job, if you were chosen for promotion, would probably be as an *area representative* for your firm, or in an equivalent post in the head office marketing department for the world-wide promotion of one particular product. In either case you would be faced with problems peculiar to different areas. A detergent, for example, sold throughout the world, will need a special approach in an African country where women have quite recently given up washing in a river and where even in towns only cold water is available on tap. Research may lead to changes in the formula so that the powder lathers readily in cold water; packaging may have to be altered to cope with heat and damp conditions and to gratify a taste for brighter colours. Where women accept hard household work, advertising may have to convey 'This product will help you do your work better' instead of – as in America and Britain – 'In your busy, car-driving, social, child-centred life you have no time to clean scum off your washing-machine – use our powder and you won't have to.'

Promotion in overseas marketing means responsibility for a larger area or more countries, or, in the brand

18      *A special display stand is often set up to draw the public's attention to the product*

divisions, for a wider range of goods. The steps might be to *area supervisor*, next *area marketing manager* and then *area marketing director*, who could be in charge of European, American, African, Australasian and Asian or Far Eastern marketing. He would allocate money, confirm campaign ideas, decide which areas offer his firm the best chance of successful sales. Right at the top comes the *international marketing director*, conferring with other directors, negotiating the whole budget of the department and deciding, with the advice of his managers, which products to concentrate on and where to try to sell them.

## Sales and sales management

Selling is the one absolutely essential part of the marketing business — without it all the research and advertising would just be useless. Selling is recognised as a skilled job and one of the few that gives a young man a chance to work away from an office desk. Indeed, even for graduates, jobs without a good deal of office work are not common.

Sales is one of the main ways into marketing, and a spell on the road is almost always part of marketing training. But even if the step into marketing is not taken, sales and sales management can offer a worthwhile and well-paid career. A salesman may work for a wholesaler or a manufacturer. He depends for continued orders upon the goodwill of his buyers. If he oversells his goods or if they are faulty in some way he will find it more difficult to sell them the next time.

After a period of initial training your first job in sales is often that of a *merchandiser*. This involves working in department stores or supermarkets looking after the interest of your firm's products, arranging displays and show cards. He may then be promoted to *salesman*. At first, you will call mainly at individual shops, armed with brochures and samples, news of special offers and discounts and new advertising about your product. He will be well briefed about his territory. If you are selling pet foods you will know how many dog licences have been issued recently, and whether there are many small flats and rooms where old people live who would be likely to have a bird or perhaps a cat for company. You will know how well-off the people in your area are, so that you can judge whether to recommend cheaper or more expensive brands of pet food. Many shopkeepers will re-order automatically and ask you to check their stock and supply what you think they need.

You will also have to find new outlets to sell your pet food — new shops, shops stocking rival brands, shops that have not before handled your goods. You need to be able to tell these retailers what advertising the product is being given, what special ingredients it has, eg extra vitamins or calcium, how well it has sold in other shops and how much profit they will make on each tin. *And* you need to persuade them to give your product a good shelf position and to put up price cards. More senior salesmen concentrate on calling at the head office of a chain of shops or supermarkets, at large department stores or at the office of a group of private grocers who have arranged to buy in bulk, and there negotiate special arrangements for supply and discount for all the shops involved. Their junior salesman would follow this up by visiting each shop.

In an efficient company the salesman's daily journeys are carefully planned so that no time is wasted but the salesman is not overtired. Nevertheless, this is an exacting job — you must have stamina as well as a company car. As a result of market research you may be selling just what people want to buy, but you still need to be determined and ebullient as well as businesslike. After all, there is probably another representative from another company waiting just outside.

While training on the job, many salesmen, whether aiming at management or not, study part-time for the examinations of the United Kingdom Commercial Travellers' Association or the Institute of Commercial and Technical Representatives. You will be paid a basic salary, but this is usually supplemented by special bonuses for particular efforts on individual products.

Above the salesmen come *field sales supervisors* or *area sales managers*. These train and supervise a group of salesmen – usually about six to eight. They plan the daily journeys of your representatives, briefing them on the whole marketing campaign, and seeing that they have brochures and all they need to make their calls. An area manager must be ready to re-assign jobs very quickly if staff are sick or special campaigns are planned. In a large firm *he* may work under a *field sales manager* who trains his supervisors and helps to forecast the expected sales of the firm's products for the future.

In charge of the sales force is usually a *general sales manager* or *director*, who liaises with the advertising, research and production managers. He will also control after-sales service to customers and technical advisory services. Salesmen, supervisors and managers who wish to move from sales divisions into marketing often prepare themselves by study for the Diploma in Marketing of the Institute of Marketing. There are also many short courses in marketing management to which companies second likely men. Those aiming at marketing jobs may move into other kinds of work – finance, market research, advertising, production – to give themselves wider experience before applying for marketing work.

Large companies, and ones selling products like toothpaste and sweets, where other brands compete aggressively, often have a *sales training officer*. Usually men are promoted to this job after successful selling and managing salesmen. It could be a step to senior sales management jobs, or, in firms where a good deal of sales training is given, it could lead to more senior jobs in this field. The sales training officer is a combination of teacher and personnel officer for salesmen. To train your salesmen to be efficient you should know the whole marketing policy of the firm and how it works. You might sit in on interviews for new salesmen, then run their initial training course, covering the products to be sold and practical demonstrations of how – and how not – to make a sale. You might also have to run refresher courses, bring sales managers up to date and, of course, keep yourself up to date on new methods of training.

This work requires good selling experience, and you should be able to explain not only which techniques work but why they work. These lessons must be clear and memorable. He should also be able to assess accurately a force of salesmen who are not under his direct control. Sales training officers are also sometimes found in the industrial marketing field, but there, like the salesmen themselves, they are usually qualified scientists, accountants or technologists.

# Industrial Marketing

Industrial marketing involves selling to manufacturers rather than to retailers, ie shops. To market goods like turbines, coal and cranes, or services like printing or canteen catering, the important thing is to be adaptable. You must tailor your product to fit the customer's needs.

Advertising it not so necessary as in consumer marketing, although many companies do produce rather restrained and dignified advertisements in technical journals and quality newspapers; this is partly a public-relations effort to improve their general image. The industrial marketer is not selling a standard product, but finding his customer, discussing what he needs and then changing his product, often very considerably, to meet the order. Some firms make a wide variety of goods in constant demand, different widths of steel tubing, for example, but their marketers will still negotiate many individual arrangements to produce a certain kind of tube in a specified quantity for a particular user — a relatively small but expensive order perhaps of very fine tubing to be used in surgery. Even so, a lot of the tubing will have to be sold to established buyers in the face of competition from other tube makers at home and abroad. So the firm's marketing men will be alert to changes in the ways of making tubes, in different kinds of steel which may be developed and in what sorts of tubes may be needed in future.

The industrial marketer must know about such new technological developments in his field while they are still at the research stage, so that he can change his own product and think up new ones accordingly. Not only must marketers in this work know all about their product, its use and how to alter it without lessening its efficiency or safety, they must also be able to work out how much all this will cost and what profit they will make. Financing such big deals is fairly complicated and for this reason many industrial marketers start as qualified accountants, mathematicians, statisticians or lawyers as well as engineers and scientists.

As an O or A level entrant, you would be likely to start in a research, production or accounting section. You should qualify by day-release or evening classes for one of the professions mentioned above, or in sales or marketing. You might then move into industrial selling, which is a more senior job than that of consumer selling. You will need experience in various branches of the firm before being ready to sell industrial goods at home or overseas. Some A level trainees and new graduates in subjects like sociology, psychology and arts are recruited, usually on general management schemes or once again as market research, statistical or other trainees. After varied experience you may move into selling or a junior post in marketing. People who already have a relevant degree, a Higher National Diploma, a professional qualification or wide business experience may be taken straight into the selling or marketing department and trained in the firm and on short external courses for this work.

Depending upon how many products the company makes, as a *junior marketing executive* your work may be divided according to the type of goods you sell or the type of industry you mainly deal with. The first is more common for the marketer, although the salesman's territory may be arranged so that selling knit-wear machinery

25

he deals mainly with hosiery manufacturers in the Nottingham area. As a *marketing services manager* you would be less concerned than your opposite number in consumer marketing with organising advertising and displays, but more with providing technical advisory services and specialised market research. You may also arrange for the firm to take a stand at industrial exhibitions and British Weeks abroad.

## Working abroad

More firms are beginning to realise that overseas marketing is not only good for Britain but also necessary for them if they are to expand any further. Selling our products abroad is not easy, particularly with industrial goods. In Germany, for example, they may be competing with a cheaper German-made article – one which may even be exported to Britain!

As in consumer marketing, British companies often have factories in other countries and use local marketers. But smaller specialist firms, making perhaps a range of complex electronic equipment, may find it easier to make the product in Britain and fly out a marketer whenever a likely customer is spotted by local salesmen or by home-based researchers. He can then make top-level arrangements to supply the right goods at the right time at an acceptable price. Other companies which make goods in more general use, mining machinery for example, may have area marketing managers in established sales areas, as in consumer marketing.

But on the whole there are in overseas industrial marketing many specialists ready to take the next flight to Beirut, Chicago, Frankfurt or Hong Kong to sell and install equipment and cope with any snags that may arise. These include *technical instructors* and *advisers* to

26

explain how to install and to use a computer, for example; *development* and *service engineers* to adapt and overhaul the machinery; *marketing research* and *design specialists* to investigate present and future needs for computers and exactly what calculations they will have to cope with, as well as various *senior executives* to discuss important deals and generally to show the flag.

## Industrial selling

Selling industrial goods is an extremely skilled job which often overlaps with marketing. Entry once again is either from other branches of business or from technical college or university, and engineers and scientists are much in demand. The salesman has a great deal of responsibility. You must be well informed and self-confident enough to discuss your product with the buyer's top management — accountants, purchasing officers, engineers and design specialists. You will have the authority to conclude many deals as your firm's delegate, and you will often have to make decisions on your own initiative. You will make a fairly small number of sales, and so cover a wide area; as you visit firms you will be expected to note any changes in their organisation or in their products, and send back this information to your own research department.

Industrial salesmen are also called *technical representatives* and *sales engineers*. Their status and pay are usually higher than those of consumer-goods salesmen in recognition of their extra qualifications and responsibilities.

Selling services also requires expert knowledge and an awareness of what is practicable. To sell a catering service to a factory, the salesman must work out how much subsidy per meal the firm will grant and how much to charge the worker; whether food is to be cooked on the premises and for how long each day it should be served;

whether a microwave oven or just hotplates will be needed; if there are many other local jobs for the part-time women workers who would staff the canteen, and a host of other questions. These special qualities and experience make the industrial salesman likely for promotion — usually to *senior sales engineer*, then *area sales manager* and then a head office job, probably in marketing. Internal and external training is similar to that for industrial marketing.

# Market Research

Nowadays this is fundamental to marketing. Of course, market research covers other fields too — what they think of the new 50-pence piece, or which political party people would vote for and why. Whatever the topic, the research will be put to practical use. Someone will have commissioned it, and the results will help this client to solve specific problems in his own work. Usually these clients are marketers.

Market research may be carried on in a separate department of a company's marketing division. This usually happens in large companies. Whether a company has a research department or not, it will probably use a market research agency, a separate organisation with its own management, which works for several clients or is possibly tied by contract to work for one large firm only. Many advertising agencies also have their own market research departments. This work has grown enormously in recent years, and few firms would try to sell a new or altered product without market-research testing first. They have too much to lose by mistakes.

Openings exist for several kinds of people. *Research assistants*, who help to plan surveys and write questionnaires, may be boys or girls with A levels or degrees in subjects like psychology, sociology, statistics and economics. Other subjects, for example, arts subjects, may be acceptable. A few firms will consider O level entrants with a good range of passes, preferably including mathematics. They and qualified specialists assist a *research officer*.

The *interviewers* are usually women. Some are married, working part-time, with a good educational background and lots of energy. Some firms take on a team of women graduates and A level girls — perhaps with some working experience — supply them with a car and send them all over the country to make surveys.

Analysis of the data is usually done by computer. Qualified *statisticians* and *systems analysts* are needed to plan the work; *programmers* (usually graduate or A level mathematicians) translate information into computer languages, and punch-card operators and other clerical workers do the more routine work.

A trainee, who starts as a research assistant, may be promoted to research officer and then *account executive*, managing all the research processes for one client or brand. You then move into management or into marketing management posts. Interviewers may be promoted to be *supervisors* of a group of interviewers. Some may break through into management, as may statisticians, psychologists and other specialists.

In consumer marketing the work involves many different surveys and practical tests; on the industrial side there are more telephone and postal enquiries.

Several methods are used in market research. If you do *desk research* you will read all the journals and press reports, trade figures and published material about a specific problem and write digests and reports. *Trade research* means checking the attitudes of the retail

*Discussing the relationship between Profit and Sales at Salford Technical College*

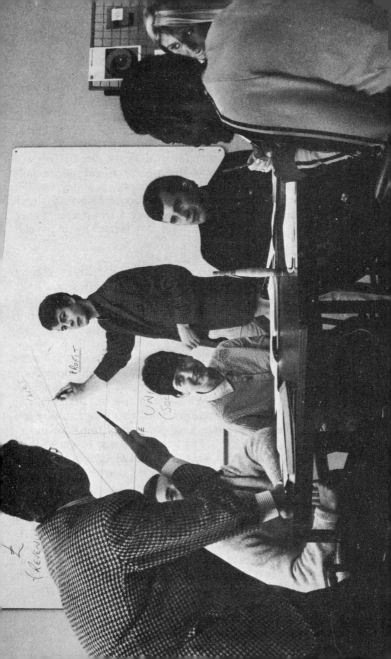

or wholesale trade to a product and how it is selling in their outlets. It includes questioning shopkeepers, talking to buyers in large organisations, carrying out store checks (which simply tell whether a shop stocks a product or not) and organising *retail audits* (which means counting stocks and deliveries to produce sales figures).

Enquiries can take the form of *depth discussions* with individuals, going into their non-rational impressions about a product. For example, lots of men may feel that deodorants are effeminate. Some cooks hate very simple cake mixes because they can make a woman feel superfluous. Such discussions are conducted by a psychologist.

But the chief and best known method of market research is the *consumer survey*, using questionnaires and interviews. The marketers' ultimate customers will probably be millions of housewives and their families, and it is obviously not practical to question them all — not even the Census covers everyone in detail — so a random sample is taken. Luckily it is a fact that the views of a few hundred people, chosen without bias, will divide proportionately in approximately the same way as those of a few thousand or millions. When the sample has been picked a questionnaire has to be drawn up. This is not an easy job, as people do not always say what they think, or indeed think what they feel. The questions have to get at these underlying feelings, which often lead people to choose products for completely unexpected reasons.

Here the psychologist, trained to be aware of the secret hopes and fears of ordinary people, can give a useful lead. If a company, for instance, wants to know whether to try to sell tea-bags as opposed to packets of loose tea in the North-east a survey will be planned. When the questionnaire is being written you could ask the housewife, 'Will you buy tea-bags if we sell them here?' and she might well say 'Yes' to get rid of the interviewer. It would probably be better to say, 'We would value your advice on tea-making. Tell us how you go about it. What tips can you offer?' Having found out which brand she uses and established her as an expert on good-quality tea, you might lead the conversation round to television or other advertisements for your own 'quality' tea in tea-bags, and probe discreetly into whether she might use them for her mid-morning tea or when she was especially busy. The questionnaire is not designed to *change* her attitudes, but rather to reveal her true feelings by posing questions in a way that will not produce a superficial or conventional answer.

The tea-bag questionnaire would be sent out with a team of interviewers, each being assigned a certain number of house calls or random street interviews. (Field interviewers might be obtained from another agency specialising in this work.) The team could well be on location for a week or more, and in spite of their cars would be likely to find the walking involved and the effort of constant new encounters fairly exhausting. While this campaign was being conducted other investigations might take place – checks with London grocers who already sell tea-bags and perhaps consultation of the shopping diaries which a group of selected housewives may keep for the company.

The results of all these researches would be sent back to the *research officer* who, together with the statisticians, would extract the information he needed from all this material. The figures are transferred on to punch cards, and the programmers, briefed by the systems analyst, prepare the computers to tabulate the information in many different ways. Then the *account executive* reports to the client firm, and makes his recommendations.

Even in industrial marketing when several firms make

similar fairly standard products like cardboard packing cases, for example, competition leads manufacturers to use market surveys, investigating what most customers require in terms of strength, weight, ease of handling and fastening and appearance. Research helps to determine cost, and to pinpoint new potential users and different kinds of boxes that the firm might profitably make.

The trained market researcher must have a knowledge of statistics, although he need not be an expert, as help is always available. Economics is also useful so that he knows what suggestions are practicable in business terms. He certainly needs some knowledge of sociology – people don't just buy things because they like them or to satisfy some hidden personal need. They also buy because their neighbours do, because buying certain things is the accepted pattern for their income group, because they are influenced by some general trend, helped along by advertising. Most of us tend to buy maxi coats or whatever at about the same time, and so how social pressures and fashions develop and change is very much a part of market research.

Training is mainly on the job, and there are naturally far more jobs for interviewers and semi-clerical workers than for executive trainees. Some entrants have already taken marketing and business studies courses, or courses like that in advertising at the College for the Distributive Trades. There are a few theoretical courses at universities and colleges which include market research, and an HND course with market research as a main option is available at Liverpool College of Commerce, but these are intended to supplement practical experience in the work. The successful market research executive needs business skill, imagination and the capacity to pay attention to detail. At the top, this work is very well paid, and it is one of the main avenues into marketing proper.

# Other work in Marketing

## Consultancy

Marketing consultants are private agents who are called in by other firms to advise on marketing problems. They are very often asked to help a firm thinking of trying to sell goods in competitive markets, in Europe or the USA, for example. Clearly this is a job for the experienced and successful marketer.

Most consultants, who specialise to some extent in the kinds of marketing they deal with, are graduates; some have studied management at colleges of technology; some have taken short marketing courses while working in the field; others have experience with manufacturing companies.

There are *assistant, consultant, senior consultant* and *senior management* posts in consultancy. Many practising marketers and college teachers of marketing are also part-time consultants.

## Teaching marketing

Now that there are so many marketing courses in universities and technical colleges, with both specialist postgraduate courses and marketing subjects taught as part of business studies courses, and as more companies set up and second staff to advanced marketing courses, there are opportunities for experienced marketers to go on to teach their subject.

In a technical college the work will be condensed, as marketing will be only one subject studied in a course by the student. In a university, however, the teacher will be concerned with the history and theory of marketing and with encouraging exercises and research in the subject. In short advanced courses, he will be helping executives to keep up to date and to review their own work objectively.

Since teachers are paid considerably less than fairly senior marketers, many marketing teachers supplement their earnings with consultancy fees. Indeed, it is necessary that they should continue to work in marketing in order to keep up to date and to retain a sense of perspective.

# Two fictional marketing and selling campaigns

These campaigns are much simplified and intended only as examples of the work involved in marketing; they include as many activities as possible. They show the sequence of events and how certain decisions are made. (Any similarity to existing products companies is entirely accidental.)

## Consumer marketing – the Primrose Margarine Campaign

**Stage 1** *Variety Foods Ltd*, manufacturers of many grocery and household products, are considering exploring the market for a new soft margarine. This product is based on recent technological advance, and only a few other brands are in the shops. One factor influencing *Variety Foods* is that if in future Britain joins the Common Market and butter prices soar this kind of margarine may well prove an acceptable alternative.

*Brand manager* appointed to co-ordinate activities.

**Stage 2** *Variety Foods Market Research Department* carry out desk research from trade journals and published statistics to find out how many people buy soft and other margarines.

*Production* – the research and development department reports on ingredients and processing of the proposed type of margarine.

*Finance* report on estimated costs of the venture.

*Board* approves further marketing efforts for Brand X margarine.

**Stage 3** *Marketing managers* go ahead with tests to decide possible composition and marketing of Brand X. Further market studies carried out by desk researchers.

*Market research* and *production* make sample margarines, differing in texture, colour, taste, size and shape of container. These samples, and some already established brands, are presented anonymously for a small number of people – often employees – to try. Their comments are taped. Sometimes they are asked simple questions ... 'Which of these two tastes is more salty? more oily? more expensive? Which of these shapes looks biggest? Which do you like best?' Results are analysed and a report made.

**Stage 4** *Marketers* eliminate some proposed recipes. *Market research* carries out more tests, concerned with the entire image of margarine. *Depth investigations* are made in discussion groups, covering problem attitudes, for example – 'Is margarine second best? Do you think it is pleasant to eat? Useful to cook with? How much would you be prepared to pay for margarine? What kind of people buy it most? What qualities do you want in this product – good spreading straight from the refrigerator, easy creaming for cake-making? In the light of all this, what do you think of Brand X?'

Reports are made, showing that people on the whole still think of margarine as a second-choice economy food, useful for cooking, but too oily and 'lower class' to be acceptable at table. However, years of advertisements for good-quality conventional margarines have undermined these attitudes to some extent and feelings are now ambivalent.

**Stage 5** *Marketers* decide to continue tests, as results seem generally favourable. Further discussions with *finance* and funds authorised for survey.

**Stage 6** *Market research agency* briefed for full-scale *survey*. Questionnaires are prepared on the basis of the questions described in Stage 4 and the sample is chosen. *Interviewers* interrogate housewives on margarine-buying habits and opinions, on prices and the most convenient packaging. Shopkeepers are questioned to find out what is sold in different kinds of shop. Housewives' shopping diary records are consulted. Results are analysed and reports made.

*Marketers* decide to launch campaign for Brand X margarine.

*Finance* bring up to date proposed budget estimates.

*Production* – research and development begin to approach a decision on ingredients and methods of manufacture.

**Stage 7** *Marketers* decide rough price, weight of packs and in which kinds of shops to sell the products – supermarkets, family grocers, departmental stores.

**Stage 8** *Marketers, market research agency, advertising agency* and *specialists from packaging firm* meet and decisions are reached on the following:

*The general image of Brand X margarine.* This is to some extent determined by the nature of its main compe-

39

titors, *Wonder* – an American product which emphasises its vegetable oil content; and *Quickspread* – an English margarine priced as low as possible, which puts its main advertising effort into its convenience factors. For example, it will spread directly from the refrigerator. Other popular margarines are conventional, and advertising tends to stress their 'buttery' taste, convenient packaging or the 'guaranteed success' of using them in cake- and pastry-making.

It is decided that *Brand X* will be a luxury margarine, costing at least a few pennies more than *Quickspread* and associated with conscientious housewives who will pay a little more for a good product. They are not well-to-do housewives, but working- and middle-class women who like to buy the best they can afford for their families. No comparison will be made with butter. *Brand X* will simply be the best margarine, although the marketers know that in the future margarine may well be bought as a substitute for very expensive butter. No mention will be made of its freedom from animal fats.

So *Brand X* is to be the best margarine – luxurious, creamy and versatile. It is to be promoted as a modern product for modern, busy people who like good food.

*Appearance and taste*. The margarine will be soft and light, creamy in texture, slightly salt and pale yellow in colour.

*Name – Primrose Margarine.*

*Packaging*. Tentative proposals are to package the margarine in square, very pale yellow plastic tubs with white and gold lids. The stylised print of a primrose should be clearly visible on the lid, which is an important feature, as the margarine will probably be displayed in low deep-freeze cabinets.

*Advertising.* It is decided that some early advertising, mainly in magazines and colour supplements, will feature the stylised primrose. Posters, TV commercials and later colour press advertisements will show poised (but not too elegant) housewives eating with their enchanting children in clean, modern, white kitchens, flooded with golden sunlight. Simple clear yellow and white colouring is all-important. The suggestion will be that ordinary housewives with healthy families can bring an extra glow to their lives by using 'the luxurious, smooth and creamy margarine – the Primrose path'.

Alternative campaigns are also planned, some brighter and brasher, some using humour and a frank approach – 'So you think margarine is vile? Ours may change your mind.' *Legal department* is to get trade-mark clearance for brand name.

**Stage 9** *Brand manager* prepares a budget for the campaign and submits it to senior management.

**Stage 10** *Advertising agency* works on poster, press advertisements, TV commercials and buys time and space for the future campaign.

*Production* and *packaging* make a small number of varied samples. They test the packages for storage, strength, ease of opening and replacing lid.

**Stage 11** *Market research* agency survey, with a smaller sample of people, the effectiveness of various advertisement pictures, captions and commercials. They also check preferences for particular types of package. Reports are made.

*Production* and *packaging* make up a limited number of the most popular samples.

*Market research* agency arrange to *test market* these in various chosen areas or shops. Report made on sales, comments and any action taken by competitors in new advertising or increased sales efforts.

**Stage 12** *Production* organise for manufacture.

*Packaging* contract made.

*Distribution* make more detailed plans on where to sell the margarine and organise delivery.

**Stage 13** *Marketers* timetable launching for early spring.

**Stage 14** *Sales managers* briefed.

*Advertising agency* prepare salesmen's brochures.

*Salesmen* confer and are informed on whole marketing effort and main selling points. The sales campaign is planned and new possible outlets discussed.

*Advertising agency* prepare shop displays for merchandisers and engage women demonstrators to spread *Primrose* margarine on biscuits for customers in large food departments. More long-term cookery demonstrations are also planned for exhibitions and women's organisations.

**Stage 15** *Sales* effort starts. *Senior salesmen* visit head offices of supermarket and grocery chains and of voluntary organisations of private grocers; they also deal with large stores' food departments. *Salesmen* visit individual grocers, supermarkets and other shops, persuading them to buy and to set up displays.

**Stage 16** *Advertising* campaign begins, aiming at saturation coverage. Small free samples are delivered to houses, with shopping vouchers for *Primrose*.

*How should these chairs be displayed is the problem here as two of Maples' young trainees discuss the intricate problems of furniture arrangement*

**Stage 17** *Market research agency* makes survey of public reactions to *Primrose* margarine, interviewing housewives and shopkeepers, and noting television viewing figures.

*Brand manager* and *finance* examine sales figures.

*Brand manager* estimates future sales and costs, considers any needed or useful modifications to the product, packaging or campaign.

## Industrial selling – Storright Shelving Systems

John Seller is a technical representative for *Storright* Shelving Ltd, a firm which makes industrial storage systems – basically metal uprights to which a variety of shelves, racks, drawers and cabinets can be fixed. Visiting a customer in Shoreditch, Seller hears of a local fire. A wholesale hardware warehouse, George Wells, Ltd, has lost all its stock and old-fashioned wooden storage bins in the fire. Seller at once rings the firm and arranges to see the manager. He finds out a bit about the firm, its turnover, stock and staffing. He arrives at the warehouse in the middle of the cleaning-up operations and he has a chance to look around. The building is late Victorian with high narrow windows and small slow lifts. It is not an ideal warehouse, and space is limited. On the other hand, there is good access and loading space for lorries delivering goods and for the firm's own vans.

The manager tells him that Mr Wells has decided to take advantage of the fire and re-organise his firm. He has called in a company of organisation and methods specialists. Seller explains that his shelving could fit any scheme and suggests that he might meet Mr Wells and the OM specialists. This is arranged, and when he goes he leaves brochures, price lists and his business card.

At this meeting a few days later Seller has already roughly planned the kinds of units the firm may need, and it is agreed that he will work with the OM analysts to draw up a report on the reorganisation. During this work the manager and foreman are both closely consulted, and the insurance assessor, anxious after one fire that the new arrangements shall be fireproof, also helps.

The specialists and Seller plan the best places for various goods to be stored. A warehouse is a clearing house for products, and all the time goods are being unloaded, stored for a long or short period, and then reloaded for delivery to shopkeepers. Products can vary in size from a half-inch screw to a dustbin and some are too heavy or bulky to be moved in the elderly lifts. Some, like deck-chairs and paraffin heaters, are seasonal goods, and will be stocked for a limited period each year. Manufacturers do not always deliver when they promise to, and so space prepared for lawnmowers might suddenly have to be converted to hold curtain rails.

*Storright* finally submit an estimate. Of course, other shelving firms, too, have been taking an interest, and other estimates are invited. Some of these are lower than *Storright*, but Mr Wells and his advisers decide that as *Storright*'s system seems the best value, and as John Seller has been working with them on the problem in an expert and businesslike way, they will accept this estimate. Mr Wells has received insurance money as compensation for fire loss, but this still is not enough to cover all his refitting costs – especially as he has also lost some business. *Storright* will have to give him credit, with his firm and capital as security. John Seller meets Mr Wells's accountants to discuss this. When the final contract for the sale of *Storright* equipment is drawn up by his firm's solicitors John Seller might also be required to explain some points to Mr Wells's solicitors, who check the contract. Then finally either Seller or a technician from his firm checks the installation of *Storright*, and makes sure that no further changes are needed.

To sell a relatively simple industrial product, John Seller needed initiative to approach the customer, good technical information about his product, authority and persuasiveness in dealing with a wide range of experts and professional men, staying power and an eye for detail in planning the system. He also needed the ability to work in a team with the analysts, an understanding of costs and profits, and a real interest in doing the best for his customer. He was helped, of course, by offering a well-researched and well-made product, but without *his* personal qualities and practical salesmanship Mr Wells might well have bought a rival system, one less suited to his real needs.

# Education and training

This section is arranged as follows: HNC and HND courses; college diplomas; examinations set by professional bodies; first degree courses and postgraduate diplomas and degrees.

## National Diplomas and Certificates

### Higher National Certificate and Diploma in Business Studies

*HNC is a part-time and HND a full-time course; they take two years full-time, three years sandwich, two years part-time.*

Courses are available at many colleges in England and Wales and provide a useful introduction to the business world. Marketing subjects may be taken as options in the courses. For HND, Marketing Options are available at forty-eight Colleges (see *A Compendium of Advanced Courses in Technical Colleges*). *Marketing in Europe* is available at Leeds College of Commerce and Sheffield Polytechnic; *International Marketing and Languages* at Bristol College of Commerce; *Marketing within the Engineering Industry* is offered at Blackburn College of Technology; *Market Research* is available at Liverpool College of Commerce, and *Design for Marketing* at Stockport College of Technology.

Candidates for entry to these courses must usually have reached the age of eighteen and either hold an Ordinary National Diploma or Certificate in Business Studies or GCE with one or more passes at A level.

### Ordinary National Certificate and Diploma in Business Studies

Courses are offered by about 100 and 250 technical colleges respectively throughout the country. They are a preparation for HND

47

and HNC courses. Entry is at sixteen years, and candidates must have GCE O level or equivalent in four subjects, including English and mathematics, or the Certificate of Office Studies with credits in English, general studies, clerical duties and one other subject.

## Scottish Higher National Diploma and Scottish Higher National Certificate

*SHND – two years full-time or three years sandwich; SHNC – one year full-time or two years part-time.*

For SHND options include *Marketing Administration.* For SHNC options include *Export Principles and Practice* and *Marketing.* SHND courses are offered at Aberdeen College of Commerce, the Scottish College of Textiles, Galashiels, and Edinburgh College of Commerce.

Candidates must hold the Scottish National Certificate in Business Studies or a direct equivalent. Candidates over twenty-one may exceptionally be eligible if they possess at least three Scottish Certificate of Education passes at Higher grade, including English, and at least two other Ordinary grade passes.

The Scottish Council for Commercial, Administrative and Professional Education, which awards the Scottish HND and HNC, also awards a *Diploma in Commerce.* This is taken after a three-year full-time course. Applicants under twenty-three must have at least one GCE A level and six O level passes or the equivalent. Marketing may be taken as a specialised option at Edinburgh College of Commerce and Dundee College of Technology.

# College Associateships, Diplomas and Certificates

*Diplomas in Marketing* are awarded after full-time courses at Birmingham College of Commerce, Cassio College, Watford, and Kingston-upon-Thames College of Technology. A part-time course is offered at West Bromwich College of Commerce and Technology.

*Diploma in International Marketing:* one year full-time course at Thurrock Technical College and at Sunderland Polytechnic.

*Diploma in Export Marketing:* full-time courses at High Wycombe College of Technology and Thurrock Technical College. A sandwich course is offered at the City of Westminster College.

*Associateship in Foreign Languages and European Marketing:* full-time course at Sheffield Polytechnic.

*Certificate in Business Computing and Marketing:* part-time course at North-Western Polytechnic, London N5.

*Diploma in Commercial Travelling:* part-time course at Chester College of Further Education.


# Diplomas and Membership examinations of professional bodies

*Diploma in Marketing of the Institute of Marketing* (*DipM*). This is the main qualification studied for by marketing trainees and others aiming at careers in this field.

The Diploma is taken after three years part-time study. Over 100 technical colleges provide tuition for day-release and evening students, and correspondence courses are also available. Candidates must be at least eighteen years old and hold GCE O level passes or the equivalent in four subjects. The courses for parts I and II of the examination are constituted as a Higher Certificate course in Marketing, equivalent to the HND in Business Studies, so those holding HND or HND in Business Studies are obviously exempt from parts I and II of the Diploma examination.

Graduates in relevant subjects may be granted exemption from corresponding subjects, as may holders of professional qualifications in advertising, export, accountancy, etc, and holders of the Senior Commercial Certificate of the former Scottish Council for Commercial Education. The examination for the Diploma covers the following subjects:

*Part I* Marketing; economics; economic geography; business history.

*Part II* Marketing; commercial law; applied statistics; accounting.

*Part III* Marketing – questions on a previously circulated case history with statistics and illustrations attached; advertising; market research.

Holders of the Diploma qualify for Graduate Membership of the Institute; those who also have some executive responsibility in their jobs may be granted Associate Membership.

The Institute has established a College of Marketing to develop Diploma and other Marketing educational work, and it runs many short courses for experienced marketers.

Other advanced short courses are run by the British Institute of Management, the Marketing Society and at business study centres such as Ashridge College.

*The Marketing Society, the Market Research Society* and *the Institution of Sales Engineers* do not conduct their own examinations but admit to membership those who work in these fields and who satisfy minimum requirements of age and of qualification by holding GCE, HND or degrees or having passed membership examinations of other related professional bodies.

*The Institute of Export.* To qualify for Associate Membership of the Institute an applicant must pass the qualifying examination which is taken in three parts.

*The Intermediate Examination* is open to Registered Students of the Institute. It covers commerce, English for commerce, commercial geography and general principles of law. *The Final Examination* is taken in two parts. Candidates for Part I must be at least eighteen and have passed the Intermediate; for Part II they must be at least thirty and have passed Part I. Part I covers export practice, principles of marketing overseas, international trade and payments, and commercial law. Part II covers export practice, principles of marketing overseas, finance of foreign trade, insurance of export cargoes and law of carriage of goods. Some exemptions may be granted for relevant qualifications.

*Institute of Commercial and Technical Representatives Ltd.* Candidates for the Institute's admission examinations must be at least eighteen years old and hold ONC in Business Studies or a similar subject or GCE O level passes in English and three other subjects. They must also have started a course of training for the examinations.

*The Intermediate Examination* covers the following subjects: the salesmen; the product; the sales interview; psychological considerations; the problem of selling; techniques of selling.

Exemptions may be granted to holders of the UCTA (United Commercial Travellers Association) Diploma in Salesmanship at credit level and Part II of the Diploma of the Institute of Marketing.

*The Final Examination.* Candidates must have passed or been exempted from the Intermediate Examination. The syllabus, which takes two years part-time study, covers advanced salesmanship; tools, techniques and methods used in advanced salesmanship; field sales organisation; appreciation of headquarters' sales organisation.

*United Commercial Travellers Association of Great Britain and Ireland (Incorporated)*. All those employed as commercial travellers may become members of the UCTA. Graduateship is open to those who hold the Association's Salesmanship Diploma but who are not yet working as commercial travellers.

*The Diploma in Salesmanship*. Candidates must be at least eighteen years old and must undertake a period of part-time study for the Diploma.

*The Preliminary Examination* is in English. Exemption is given for a GCE O level or equivalent pass in English.

*The Final Examination* covers salesmanship and sales organisation. Parts of the examination may be taken in successive years.

# First degrees, postgraduate diplomas and degrees in Marketing

## First degrees in Marketing

Woolwich Polytechnic. BA (Council for National Academic Awards (CNAA)) in International Marketing. Four-year sandwich course.

Huddersfield College of Technology. BA (CNAA) in Textile Marketing. Four-year sandwich course.

## Postgraduate diplomas in Marketing

Ealing Technical College. Diploma in Management and Marketing Studies. One year full-time.

High Wycombe College of Technology. Diploma in Export Marketing. Two years part-time.

Strathclyde University. Diploma in Marketing. One year full-time.

## Postgraduate degrees in Marketing

*Higher degrees awarded after research work*

Lancaster University. MSc or DPhil in Marketing.

*Higher degrees awarded after a course of instruction*

City University. MSc in Industrial Marketing. One year full-time.

Lancaster University. MA in Marketing. One year full-time.

Salford University. MSc in Marketing Management. One year full-time.

Strathclyde University. MSc in Marketing. One year full-time.

# First degrees, postgraduate diplomas and degrees in Business Studies and Management Studies

## First degree courses including Marketing, Business Studies and Management Studies

Aston University. BSc in Administrative Science. Four years sandwich.

Bath University. BSc in Economics and Administration. Four years sandwich.

Birmingham University. BCom in Commerce. Three years full-time.

Bradford University. BSc in Business and Administrative Studies. Three years full-time.

Brighton College of Technology. BA (CNAA) in Business Studies. Four years sandwich.

City of London College. BA (CNAA) in Business Studies. Four years sandwich.

Dagenham – Barking Regional College of Technology. BA (CNAA) in Business Studies. Four years sandwich.

Ealing Technical College. BA (CNAA) in Business Studies. Four years sandwich.

Edinburgh University. BCom in Commerce (Honours course). Four years full-time. BSc (Ordinary course) Business Studies option can include Marketing. Three years full-time. BSc(SocSci) (Ordinary course) Business Studies option can include Marketing. Three years full-time.

Enfield College of Technology. BA (CNAA) in Business Studies. Four years sandwich.

Hatfield Polytechnic. BA (CNAA) in Business Studies. Four years sandwich.

Lancaster University. BA in Financial Control. Three years full-time.

Lanchester College of Technology, Coventry. BA (CNAA) in Business Studies. Four years sandwich.

Manchester University (Faculty of Technology). BSc in Management Sciences. Three years full-time.

Portsmouth College of Technology. BA (CNAA) in Business Studies. Four years sandwich.

Regent Street Polytechnic, London W1. BA (CNAA) in Business Studies. Four years sandwich. BSc (CNAA) in Commerce with Engineering. Four years sandwich.

Sheffield University. BA or BEng in Economics and Business Studies. Three years full-time. BA in Economics, Business Studies and Accountancy and Financial Administration. Three years full-time.

Strathclyde University. BA in Business and Administration. Three to four years full-time.

Surrey University. BSc in Home Economics. Four years sandwich.

University of Wales (Institute of Science and Technology). BSc in Economics. Three years full-time.

Warwick University. BA in Management Sciences. Three years full-time. (Course includes Market Research.)

Wolverhampton College of Technology. BA (CNAA) in Business Studies. Four years sandwich.

## Postgraduate degrees including Marketing, Business Studies and management Studies

*Higher degrees awarded for research work*
Aston University. MSc or PhD in Industrial Administration.

Queen's University, Belfast. MSc or PhD in Business Studies.

Bradford University. MSc or MTech or PhD in Management.

Heriot-Watt University. MAdmin or PhD in Administrative Studies.

Lancaster University. PhD in Operational Research.

London University (Imperial College). MPhil or PhD in Operational Research and Management Studies.

Manchester School of Business Studies. PhD in Business Studies.

Manchester University (Faculty of Technology). MSc or PhD in Management Sciences.

Nottingham University. MA or PhD in Industrial Economics.

*Higher degrees awarded after a course of instruction*

Aston University. MSc in Industrial Administration. One year full-time.

Birmingham University. MSocSc in Social Sciences. One to two years full-time, two years part-time.

Bradford University. MSc or Diploma in Industrial Administration in Management and Industrial Administration. One year full-time.

City University. MSc in Industrial Relations and Personnel Management. One year full-time. MSc in Managerial Economics. One year full-time.

Edinburgh University. MSc(SocSc) in Management Studies. Two years full-time.

Glasgow University. MAdmin in Administration. Two years full-time.

Heriot-Watt University. MAdmin in Administrative Studies. One to two years full-time.

Lancaster University. MA in Operational Research. One year full-time.

Liverpool University. MBA in Business Administration. Two years full-time. BPhil in Business Studies. One to two years full-time.

London University (Graduate School of Business Studies). MSc in Business Studies. Two years full-time.

London University (Imperial College). MSc or DIC (Diploma of Imperial College) in Operational Research and Management Studies. One year full-time.

54

Loughborough University. MSc in Industrial Engineering and Management. One year full-time. MSc in Economics and Administration in the Petroleum Industry. One year full-time.

Manchester University (Faculty of Technology). MSc in Management Studies. One to two years full-time.

Strathclyde University. MBA in Business Administration. One year full-time or two years part-time. MSc in Industrial Administration. One year full-time.

Warwick University. MSc in Management and Business Studies. One year full-time. MSc in Management Science and Operational Research. One year full-time.

*Postgraduate diplomas and certificates which include Marketing Studies*

Brighton College of Technology. Diploma in Management Studies. One year full-time.

Ealing Technical College. Diploma in Management Studies. One year full-time, two years part-time.

Heriot-Watt University. Diploma in Administrative Studies. One year full-time.

High Wycombe College of Technology. Management Studies. Three years part-time.

Liverpool College of Commerce. Diploma in Management Studies. One year full-time, two years part-time.

Manchester University (School of Business Studies). Diploma in Business Administration (DipBA). One year full-time.

Oxford University. Certificate in Management Studies. One year full-time.

Portsmouth College of Technology. Diploma in Management Studies. Two years full-time.

Rutherford College, Newcastle. Diploma in Management Studies. One year full-time, three years part-time.

Salford University. Diploma in Management Studies (Diploma in Advanced Studies). One to two years full-time.

Sheffield University. Diploma in Business Studies. One year full-time.

Sheffield College of Technology. Diploma in Management Studies. One year full-time.

Slough College of Technology. Diploma in Management Studies. One year full-time, two to three years part-time.

North Staffordshire College of Technology, Stoke-on-Trent. Diploma in Management Studies. One year full-time.

Strathclyde University. Diploma in Business Management. One year full-time. Diploma in Industrial Management. One year full-time.

University of Wales (Institute of Science and Technology). Diploma in Administrative Studies. One year full-time.

Waltham Forest College of Technology. Diploma in Management Studies. One year full-time.

Watford College of Technology. Diploma in Advertising Administration. Two years full-time.

Woolwich Polytechnic. Diploma in Management Studies. Two to three years part-time.

For further details of courses, you should ask your Youth Employment Officer. You can find the addresses of colleges and universities in *Directory of Further Education* published by Cornmarket Press Limited.

# Salaries

This is a rough indication of what marketers and salesmen might expect to earn at various stages of their careers. Management salaries are usually related to the company's turnover — how much money the firm spends and earns. Salesmen are paid commission on the sales they make, and often fringe benefits like cars and first-class travel passes supplement basic salaries.

## Marketing

Starting salaries for marketing trainees in retail or consumer work will range from £1000 to £1500 a year. A Brand Manager in his middle twenties might earn between £1500 and £2500 a year. Marketing Service Managers and Marketing Managers may earn, according to the responsibilities they have, up to £5000 and £7500 respectively. Marketing Directors in large companies would probably earn over £10,000 a year, sometimes well over.

Overseas Marketers, especially those of industrial goods, can earn £3500–£4000 by the time they are thirty.

An International Marketing Director would earn at least £4500, but for senior executives — managers and directors — salaries can range up to £10,000 a year.

## Sales

A Merchandiser earns about £800 a year.

A Salesman earns up to £1600 a year, and more senior Salesmen earn up to £2000 a year.

Key Salesmen or Sales Supervisors may earn up to £3000 a year.

Field Sales Managers may earn £2000–£3000 a year, but senior managers in large companies may earn well over £3000, up to £10,000 a year or more.

Sales Training Officers are usually paid between £1500 and £3500 according to the emphasis placed on training in their company.


## Market Research

Starting salaries for trainees are about £1000–£1500 a year.

A Marketing Consultant or Manager of a Research Department may earn £2000–£3000 a year or more.

Senior Managers can earn salaries up to and above £10,000 a year.

Interviewers are paid 35s. to £3 a day.

Clerical workers in analysis are paid the normal rate for this type of work and very often above.

## Teachers of Marketing

Teachers in technical colleges are paid on the Burnham scale – Lecturers £1110–£2417, Senior Lecturers £2417–£2752. With Head of Department or other extra responsibility they may earn up to £4000. University lecturers are paid £1240–£2850 a year, professors £3780–£4675.

## Applying for a job

A brief word on this is necessary, because Marketing is a highly competitive field of work. The following are the most important points:

1 Make sure you are as well qualified as possible – you may be able to take a further specialist course.
2 Find out about firms with training schemes – from the *Cornmarket Directories* or the *CRAC Yearbook* (listed below, page 62), from the Press, including the trade journals at the library, and also from professional careers advisers.
3 Apply in writing to as many of these firms as seem suitable; many marketers recommend writing 50–100 letters.
4 Be open-minded about where you work. You may well have to live away from home.
5 Prepare for your interview by reading about the firm and what it makes. Be clear about what you have to offer.

You may be interested in the results of a quick check I made of a few firms with training schemes.

## Marketing

Of 67 firms with training schemes:

> 25 offer commercial apprenticeships to O level entrants.
> 37 seek A level or OND candidates to work part-time for HND or a degree.
> 53 seek graduates. Of these 31 normally take men only.

## Market Research

Of 15 firms offering executive training:

> None takes O level entrants.
> Two seek A level and OND entrants.
> 13 take graduates only. Of these four take men only.

## Sales and Sales Management

Of 90 firms with training schemes:

> 51 take O level entrants.
> 54 take A level and OND entrants.
> 54 take graduates. Of these 36 take men only.

This is, of course, a very rough guide, and can only indicate the relative frequency of opportunities; there are, for example, a small number of openings in Market Research for O level entrants.

# Further information

For further details of courses, you should ask your Youth Employment Officer. You can find the addresses of colleges and universities in *Directory of Further Education* published by Cornmarket Press Limited.

## Useful addresses

Institute of Commercial and Technical Representatives, Ltd, Sardinia House, 52 Lincoln's Inn Fields, London WC2

The Institute of Export, Export House, 14 Hallam Street, London WIN 6HT

The Institute of Marketing, Richbell Place, Lamb's Conduit Street, London WC1

The Institution of Sales Engineers, 22 Vicarage Fields, Warwick

The Marketing Society, 8 Clifden House, Windmill Road, Brentford, Middlesex

The Market Research Society, 39 Hereford Street, London W1

United Commercial Travellers Association of Great Britain and Ireland (Incorporated), Knutsford, Cheshire

## Bibliography

### General publications

The Cornmarket Press, 42/43 Conduit Street, London W1R ONL:
*Which University*
*Directory of Postgraduate Courses and Opportunities*
*Directory of Opportunities for Graduates*
*Directory of Further Education*
*Careers for School Leavers*

*Kogan Page, 16 Gray's Inn Road, London WC1:*
*The Industrial Training Yearbook*
*British Qualifications*
*Industry and Careers* D E Wheatley, Iliffe
*Careers Research and Advisory Centre (CRAC) Yearbook*

## Books on Marketing, Sales and Market Research

*Marketing* Colin Melver, Pan Piper
*Careers in Marketing* An Institute of Marketing Review, Pan Piper
*An Introduction to Marketing* Smallbone, Staples Press
*Marketing and the Brand Manager* Metcalf, Pergamon Press
*Marketing and Market Research* Adler, Crosby Lockwood
*Directory of British Market Research Organisation and Services*
Adler, Crosby Lockwood
*Teach Yourself Market Research* K Dyce Sharp, Institute of Export
*The Market Research Society Yearbook*
*Professional Salesmanship* Cyril Hudson, Staples Press
*Professional Sales Organisation* Cyril Hudson, Staples Press (in preparation)
*Sales Management* M J P Baynes, Robert Hale Ltd
*Handbook of Sales Training* National Sales Executives Inc, available from the Institute of Marketing
*Teach Yourself Exporting* Taylor and Rutland, and *Marketing Overseas* H Deschampsneufs, both available from the Institute of Export
*Advertising* – a general introduction Caplan, Business Publications and IPA


## Journals

*Marketing* – Institute of Marketing
*Admap* Cornmarket Press
*Advertisers' Weekly* Haymarket Press
*Campaign* Haymarket Press


Other Institutions mentioned above also have their own journals which provide useful information.